CON

FIRST COURSES

VEGETABLE DISHES AND GARNISHES

CAKES, SWEETMEATS, ETC.

INTRODUCTION

"There will be a day in which killing an animal will be considered as killing a human being."

Leonardo da Vinci

"What do we eat today? Rabbit? But a rabbit can't be eaten, it's an animal!"

Marilena, 4 years old
(Marilena is the author's niece)

Since I began to collect the recipes for my book *Le ricette della mi' nonna* (Sarnus, 2012), some years have passed. The title of that book is not a catch phrase, but just the truth. The book arose from the need to preserve the ancient gastronomic knowledge that has been transmitted through the generations up to my family. So, as dictated by my Grandmother, who was the last person of my family who knew such knowledge, I wrote the recipes, and I took photographs of a part of them prepared by her. My Grandma, her name Giovannina Nencini (1921-2014), was born in Mugello (Tuscany, Italy) near Florence, and was a housewife with a lifelong passion for cooking.

In the meanwhile, my relationship with food has deeply evolved, in particular in 2013 I converted to veganism, either for animal ethic reasons, or for human health reasons. So, I decided to extract from *Le ricette della mi' nonna* a vegan version for those who follow this diet, but nevertheless love also traditional Italian cousin, Tuscan particularly. It is notable that many traditional Tuscan recipes are vegan just as they are, for example Ribollita, Castagnaccio, Fagioli all'uccelletto, etc., whereas small modifications are enough to make some others vegan. For example, Piselli alla fiorentina are made with a small quantity of bacon that can be eliminated without to compromise the taste significantly.

This book contains only the latter kind of recipe. In cakes and sweet things cow's milk and butter have been replaced with vegetable ones, or more simply, with olive oil. Eggs have been directly eliminated. Obviously, small variations in taste may occur, but in my experience there is nothing to lose, rather the opposite is often true. Anyway, if one has chosen to be vegan, must be ready to accept some compromises with taste! I recall that there exist also recipes made vegan in a much more demanding way, for instance Braciole di manzo, Peposo, Spezzatino di manzo, Zuccotto, or even Bistecca, for which I refer the reader to the specialized publications already available.

The explanations of the recipes are essential, the quantities of the ingredients are for four people, and are only approximated: each one adjusts them to his requirements. The recipes that have been made vegan are completed with a footnote in which I explain how I made it. When I mention olive oil, I always mean extra virgin olive oil of excellent quality.

Fabrizio Baroni

PRAISE OF TUSCAN BREAD

I write this brief note because if you do not have any Tuscan bread available, you can anyway choose for a kind of bread as similar as possible to it. The typical Tuscan bread is simple and rustic bread with a large and round shape. It is characterized by the lack of salt, and the ingredients are wheat flour, water and brewer's yeast only. It is preferably cooked in wood-burning oven, and this way it can be preserved for about a week. In Tuscany cookery, bread has always been playing a central role, either fresh to accompany every kind of food like olive oil, beans, jams, fruit, etc., or stale as an ingredient in a lot of traditional recipes like, for example, the famous Ribollita. In fact, for instance, my family uses to eat almost every food with bread, and Tuscans call all foods different from bread "companatico", that means literally every food "that accompanies bread". Bread is truly one of the pillars of traditional cookery in Tuscany.

STARTERS

FETTE DI CAVOLO NERO
Bread slice with kale

4 slices of homemade Tuscan bread
2 bunches of dark green cabbage or kale
1 garlic clove - Excellent olive oil, freshly pressed
Salt and pepper

Wash the cabbage leaves (possibly that have "felt" the cold winter nights) and boil them in already boiling salted water for about 20 minutes. It is better to start with already warm water in order to minimize the time of immersion of the cabbage, so that it preserves its substances much as possible. The same applies to the other vegetables. Toast the slices of bread, preferably a little stale, rub with a peeled clove of garlic and moisten with the stock of the cabbage, still hot. Lay one or more squeezed cabbage leaves on each slice and season with plenty of oil, salt and pepper. They are served hot, and, in spite of the simplicity of the recipe, the taste is amazing!

FETTUNTA
Bread slices with oil

4 slices of fresh homemade bread - 1 garlic clove
Excellent olive oil, freshly pressed - Salt and pepper

Toast the slices of bread on both sides until they are wonderfully crunchy and rub with a peeled clove of garlic on both sides. Season them with olive oil, salt and pepper. The slices should be eaten when the bread is still warm. A similar recipe we like to remember is *bread with oil*, which is nothing more than a slice of fresh bread seasoned with oil and salt, ideal for snacks.

FIORI DI ZUCCA FRITTI[1]
Fried courgettes flowers

16 courgette flowers - Flour, 150 g - Olive oil for frying - Salt

Wash the courgette flowers, remove the pistil and dry with a cloth. Pass them in a batter made with water and flour, and fry a few at a time until they are well golden in hot oil: take them out as they are ready with a perforated spatula depositing them on

---

[1] Traditional frying requires the addition of eggs to the butter.

an adsorbent paper towels, salting them to taste. Flowers can be fried just floured.

In May in Italy (in other countries it could be in other months) you can go around for walking in parks and campaigns and collect acacia flowers, that you can eat directly row or can follow this recipe to cook them.

INSALATA DI RISO

Rice salad

Parboiled rice, 350 g - Tomatoes, 100 g
Boiled peas, 50 g - Peppers, 100 g
Pitted green and black olives, 50 g
Pickled cucumbers and carrots, 50 g
A bunch of chives - A few leaves of basil
Olive oil - Salt and pepper

Boil the rice and drain it. Chop the basil leaves and the chives, cut the other vegetables into pieces and add them to the rice. Add a little oil, salt and pepper according to taste and let the salad stand in the refrigerator. Serve fresh, or at room temperature depending on the season.

Of course, a rice salad can be customized to taste and the ingredients and quantities in the recipe are only estimates. Also, if you replace rice with spelt you get a nice spelt salad.

PANE FRITTO[2]

Fried bread

4 slices of slightly stale bread - Olive oil for frying - Salt

This is a good way to reuse stale bread. Simply slice it, and fry the slices. Drip them and put to dry on an absorbent paper towels: salt to taste. You can also directly fry bread without batter.

This recipe, like so many others published here, is a great way to recycle leftover bread.

Fritta l'è bona anch'una ciabatta!

Even a fried slipper is good!

PANE, OLIO E POMODORO

Bread, oil and tomato

4 slice of fresh homemade bread - 2 ripe tomatoes - Olive oil
Salt and pepper

Wash the tomatoes, cut them in half and rub on the bread slices. If you do not like the tomato seeds, you can remove them

[2] See the recipe of fiori di zucca fritti.

before rubbing. Season with plenty of oil, salt and pepper. To make the slices more substantial you can also cut thin slices of tomato and lay them on top of the slices. This is a delicious summer snack.

PINZIMONIO

Oil dip

4 artichokes - 2 fennel bulbs
2 celery stalks - 4 long baby onions
Lemon juice - Olive oil
Salt and pepper

Prepare the vegetables in the following way. Remove the hardest outer leaves of the artichokes, and when you will eat the remaining ones remove the thorn. Cut off the hardest stalks of the fennels and slice the "heart" lengthwise. Eliminate the beards of the onions and remove both the ends of the celery. Wash all parts freshly prepared and dry them well. Prepare plenty of oil in a bowl with lemon juice, salt and pepper, dip in the vegetables and bite them!

SALVIA FRITTA
Fried sage

A handful of large leaves of sage - Flour, 100 g
Olive oil for frying - Salt

Dredge the leaves of sage in a batter made with water and flour, and fry in plenty of hot oil. Take them out when they are golden, place them to dry on an absorbent paper towels and salt to taste.

Sage leaves can also be fried directly without batter until they become crisp, but be careful they do not turn black, otherwise they become bitter.

Some nice large basil leaves can also be fried the same way.

SAUCES AND STOCKS

BRODO VEGETALE
Vegetable stock

1 carrot - 1 red onion - 1 celery stalk - 1 garlic clove
4 ripe cherry tomatoes - Parsley - Salt-

Put vegetables chopped into small pieces to boil, starting from cold water for about an hour, with a pinch of salt: the stock is ready.

It is noteworthy that from vegetables alone, you can get an intensity of flavor that, at least in our opinion, is not inferior to what you can get using meat also. To enhance the result, you can remove the boiled vegetables from the stock and squeeze them with a fork on the bottom of a colander. The vegetable stock can be used to cook soups and in the preparation of courses that require the addition of liquid parts, such as rice, or it can be tasted hot alone as an invigorating drink.

CONSERVA DI POMODORO
Tomato preserve

Ripe Florentine ribbed tomatoes, about 2 kg

Among the many varieties of tomatoes, if you have it available, we suggest you use the juicy Florentine ribbed tomato. Blanch tomatoes in boiling water and press them through the tomato crusher that separates the pulp from the peel. Put the pulp in a saucepan and bring to the boil for a short time. Place a clean cloth over a colander of appropriate size and pour the hot pulp in, letting it strain through the fabric for about a quarter of an hour. Put the filtered pulp in hermetic seal glass jars and put them to boil in a water bath for about 20 minutes. Tomato preserve is basically a homemade tomato concentrate that can be very useful in many recipes. Please note that a small amount is enough to flavor a course!

Antique preparation for solid preserve: press the blanched tomatoes in the tomato crusher. Stretch out a cloth between two chairs, after having washed it in vinegar, and pour over the past. Wait for about 2 days until it is well drained and then put to dry in the oven at a low temperature until it loses all moisture. Store it in tightly sealed glass jars.

SALSA DI POMODORO

Tomato sauce

Ripe Florentine ribbed tomatoes, 1 kg - 1 carrot - 1 red onion
1 celery stalk - 2 garlic cloves - A sprig of basil - 1 chili pepper
Olive oil - Salt

As in the previous recipe, we recommend using Florentine ribbed tomato if they are available. Cut the tomatoes in halves, remove the seeds and the inner part, chop into small pieces and place in a pan. Add chopped carrot, onion, and celery without leaves, garlic and basil, add chopped chili pepper without seeds, pour a little olive oil, salt and put to boil over a low heat for about an hour.

Storage: put tomato sauce into glass jars and pour a little oil, so that it forms a sort of natural cap. Close the jars well, and after that you reopen one, you store it in the fridge. Use the sauce to flavor a good course of pasta (350 g for four people), adding some coarsely chopped basil leaves: sprinkle with grated Parmesan cheese.

This sauce can be used to dress pasta adding a few basil leaves chopped at the last moment in order to enhance the fragrance.

SALSA VERDE[3]

Green sauce

Drained pickled capers, 40 g - A bunch of parsley, 50 g
A sprig of basil - Garlic (see below) - Olive oil
Salt and pepper

Chop the herbs very finely, add only a quarter of garlic clove, otherwise it will tend to dominate in the flavor of the sauce. Add plenty of olive oil stirring well, salt and pepper.

This sauce can be used also for dressing pasta, or it can be spread on slices of fresh bread.

---

[3] Traditional green sauce contains boiled eggs and anchovy fillets.

FIRST COURSES

GNOCCHI DI FARINA GIALLA[4]

Cornmeal dumplings

Cornmeal flour, 300 g - Tomato sauce (see recipe) - Salt

Put lightly salted water to boil in a pot (the proportion of a liter of water for every 250 g of flour). Add cornmeal flour into the boiling water, stirring constantly to prevent lumps forming. Continue cooking for half an hour, always stirring, to prevent it sticking and burning on the bottom of the pot. When cooked, make the "dumplings" by taking the cornmeal with a wet tablespoon, and put them on plates alternating with layers of tomato sauce.

GNOCCHI DI PATATE (TOPINI)

Potato dumplings

Floury potatoes, 1 kg - Flour, 250 g (in addition to that necessary for dusting the pastry board) - Salt

Potato dumplings are known to Tuscan also as "topini" (little mice). Boil potatoes and peel them: transfer them to a large bowl and begin to mash gradually adding the flour, until you obtain a firm but not sticky dough that must not stick to your

[4] Making this recipe vegan consists merely in doing without grated Parmesan. Another traditional seasoning is meat sauce, whose vegan version is not here contemplated.

fingers. Take small pieces of the dough with your wet hands, roll them on a clean floury cloth until you get some "sticks" of about 1 cm in diameter, then chop in rods to make the dumplings.

Cooking: put the dumplings in salted boiling water, wait until they come to the surface and the water returns to the boil. At this point, the cooking is finished: take them out with the skimmer dripping, and season to taste.

Be careful, because the cooking time is very short. You can dress "topini" simply with vegetable butter or any sauce, for example tomato sauce or green sauce (see recipes).

MINESTRA DI FAGIOLI

Bean soup

Fresh Cannellini beans, 500 g - Striped short pasta, 200 g
1 garlic clove - Rosemary - Sage - Olive oil - Salt

Put the beans to boil from cold water with a few leaves of sage and salt for about 2 hours, and make sure to cover the pot and keep the fire as low as possible: when they are boiled pass them through a food mill and re-put the paste back into the pot. Fry the whole clove of garlic and the chopped rosemary in a little oil. Removed the garlic, add the fried oil to the mashed beans, add water as needed, so that the soup is neither too liquid nor too firm, and cook the pasta in it. Some people prefer not to mash all the legumes, but leave some whole, to make more attractive the course.

The same procedure applies to chickpeas soup: ingredients and doses are the same, replacing the fresh beans with 300 g of dried chickpeas previously soaked for at least 8 hours. Boil the chickpeas, pass them through a food mill, add the fried oil, and enough water to cook the pasta.

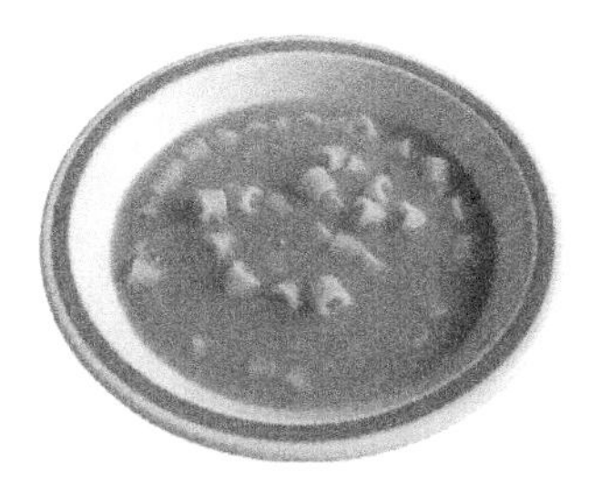

MINESTRA DI PANE

Bread soup

Stale homemade Tuscan bread, 250 g
Cannellini beans, 500 g - 2 potatoes
2 courgettes - Half a savoy cabbage
1 leek - 2 carrots
1 red onion - 1 celery stalk
A bunch of black cabbage or kale
1 garlic clove
Tomato pulp, 50 g
Olive oil - Salt

Pass the boiled beans through a food mill, but leave a small part of them whole: pour the past into the cooking water of the beans. Fry onion, garlic, leek, 1 carrot and celery. When it is browned, add the other carrot chopped into chunks. Add the past beans with their water, the whole beans and the tomato pulp. Bring gently to the boil, then add black cabbage or kale, savoy cabbage, potatoes and courgettes chopped into small pieces, and leave to simmer for about 2 hours, dosing the salt. Finally, slice thinly the bread, add it and stir until to get a soup. Let the soup rest at least for the time between a meal and the other, and then warm it up for 10 minutes before serving. The taste leaves people astonished.

This soup is very similar to "ribollita", which is nothing that left-over bread soup re-boiled.

MINESTRA DI PORRI

Leek soup

Leeks, 1 kg - Vegetable stock (see recipe), 1,5 l
Tomato pulp - Olive oil
Salt and pepper

Trim the leeks, cut into thin washers and cook in the vegetable stock with a little tomato pulp (very little!) and oil for about half an hour. Salt, and the soup is ready.

When you serve this soup, you can add some toasted slices of stale homemade bread rubbed with a pared clove of garlic, which makes this simple course more pleasant. Make this dish vegan consists only in doing without a sprinkling of grated Parmesan cheese.

MINESTRONE

Vegetable soup

2 potatoes - 3 courgettes - Half a savoy cabbage
Shelled green peas, 150 g - A small bunch of black cabbage
A bunch of chard - 1 leek - 1 carrot - 1 red onion
2 celery coasts - Salt and pepper

Wash the vegetables, cut into small pieces and put to boil slowly in salted water for about an hour, starting from cold. Add salt and pepper and stir often with a wooden spoon.

This soup can be tasted directly, even warm or cold, or you can cook some striped short pasta or rice in, or you can dip some toasted slices of bread in. If you pass it through a food mill, you get a good vegetable puree *that can be used to make soups by cooking pasta in it.*

PANZANELLA

Bread salad

Stile homemade Tuscan bread, 500 g - 1 red onion - 1 cucumber
Drained pickled capers, 30 g - Basil - Vinegar - Olive oil
Salt and pepper

Panzanella is a typical summer course. Put the bread (preferably very stale) to soak in water for about half an hour, squeeze it well, crumble and place in a bowl. Take care to squeeze the bread out well, otherwise panzanella remains wet and, even worse, leaves a deposit of water in the bottom of the bowl. This is the main possible failure of this course. Chop onion and cucumber not too finely, and add them to the soaked bread. Add whole capers, chopped basil and season with vinegar, salt, pepper and a drizzle of oil. If you have time, put in the fridge and serve cold.

Traditional panzanella just want bread, onion, ripe tomato and basil, but as it is also evident from this recipe, it is customary to personalize and enrich it at will, for example with lettuce, pitted olives, etc.

PAPPA AL POMODORO

Tomato and bread soup

Stale homemade Tuscan bread, 300 g
Ripe Florentine ribbed tomatoes, 300 g - Vegetable stock, 1 l
3 garlic cloves - Basil - Olive oil - Salt and pepper

Among tomato varieties, if available, you should use Florentine ribbed tomatoes: wash them, cut in half, remove the seeds, cut into small pieces and put to boil in stock with garlic, basil and a bit of salt for about half an hour on a medium flame. Meanwhile, cut the bread into small pieces, or thin slices, trying to crumble the crust. Add the bread to the cooking tomato and continue to boil for another 10 minutes stirring, until the bread becomes a mush. Let it rest for about 20 minutes, to "revive" the bread: at the time of serving, season with olive oil of excellent quality.

The correct quantity of tomato to the bread is very variable. Someone really likes this soup very red with a lot of tomato, someone else likes an almost imperceptible quantity. Decide according to your taste. Someone cooks the tomato in water, but with vegetable stock the result is much richer.

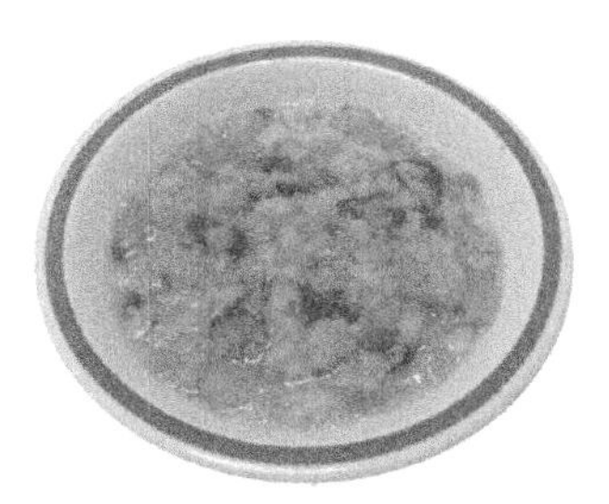

PASTE AL BURRO[5]

Pasta with butter

Short pasta, 350 - Soy butter - Salt and pepper

Trivial recipe, but how do not remember it? The classic piece of butter made directly dissolve on the pasta immediately after draining completed, for those who like, with a sprinkle of black pepper.

Soy butter may be replaced by other vegetable butters or olive oil.

---

[5] Soy, or in general vegetable, butter is in place of the cow's one, and the sprinkle of Parmesan cheese has been eliminated.

PASTE AL SUGO DI CIPOLLE

Pasta with onion sauce

Short pasta, 350 g - 2 onions - Olive oil - Salt

Peel the onions, removing the outer skin and the roots. Cut them into very thin slices and place them to sweat in oil into a covered saucepan, without letting them turn brown. Cook slowly for about half an hour, dosing salt and adding a little water or vegetable stock if necessary, until them become homogeneous. At this point they are ready for seasoning the pasta, which in the meantime you will have cooked and drained.

PASTE AL SUGO DI MELANZANE

Pasta with aubergine sauce

Short pasta, 350 g - 1 aubergine
1 garlic clove - Tomato pulp
1 chili pepper - Parsley
Basis - Olive oil - Salt

Peel the aubergine, cut into thin slices and lay down in a deep tray, covered with salt (coarse), for a few hours. Then wash the salt off, dry the slices well and brown on both sides in a pan with 4 tablespoons of olive oil over high heat. Chop garlic, parsley, basil and pepper, put on the fire in a saucepan with a film of oil. Add a table spoon of tomato pulp and the browned aubergine, dosing the salt. Cook over medium heat for a quarter of an hour, stirring. At this point the aubergine should have almost disintegrated, forming a quite thick paste. Season the pasta with this sauce.

PASTE AL SUGO DI PORCINI

Pasta with porcino mushrooms sauce

Long pasta, 350 g - Porcino mushrooms, 500 g - 1 garlic clove
Catmint - Olive oil - Salt

Prepare the mushrooms sauce following the recipe for sautéed porcino mushrooms (see recipe), but this time you have to chop the mushrooms very finely. If you like, leave some strips to make the course more attractive. Garnish the pasta with this sauce.

POLENTA
Cornmeal

Corn flour, 300 g - Salt

As mentioned in the recipe for cornmeal dumplings, put lightly salted water to boil in a large saucepan (the proportion is a liter of water for 250 g of flour). Add the cornmeal to the boiling water, stirring constantly to prevent lumps forming. Continue cooking for about 40 minutes, always stirring, otherwise the paste might stick and burn to the bottom of the pot. When cooked, the polenta should have become firm, so pour it onto a cloth, cover and let it cool before enjoying.

To taste polenta, you can cut it into slices using a wire held taut between your hands and eat it just as it is, hot or cold. But there are so many ways to dress it to make it more appetizing. We mention 2 of them: with tomato sauce (see recipe) or with some nice boiled dark green cabbage, or kale, leaves and a drizzle of oil.

RISO AI CARCIOFI
Rice with artichokes

Rice, 300 g - 4 small violet artichokes, 300 g - 1 garlic clove
Parsley - Olive oil - Salt and pepper

Remove the tough outer leaves from the artichokes, trim the tops and chop finely them, also using the tender part of the stems, with garlic and parsley. Fry in a little oil for a few minutes, add a little hot water (or vegetable stock), and cook for a quarter of an hour. Then add the rice with the hot water needed for cooking (or vegetable stock for an even tastier result), dose salt and pepper. Just before serving, make sure that the course is not too liquid, and not even too dry.

RISO AI PORCINI
Rice with porcino mushrooms

Rice, 300 g - Porcino mushrooms, 500 g - 1 garlic clove - Parsley
Olive oil - Salt and pepper

Prepare the mushrooms sauce following the recipe for *sautéed porcino mushrooms*, but this time the mushrooms have to be chopped very fine, eventually leaving only a few larger pieces to embellish the presentation of the dish. Then add the rice with the water needed for cooking.

RISO AI PORRI
Rice with leeks

Rice, 300 g - 4 leeks - 1 garlic clove - Parsley - Olive oil
Salt and pepper

Peel the leeks and chop finely with garlic and parsley, sauté for a few minutes in a little oil, add a little hot water (or vegetable stock) and cook for a quarter of an hour. Then add the rice with the hot water needed for cooking (or vegetable stock for a tastier result), dosing salt and pepper. Also in this case, make sure that the course, just before serving, is not too liquid, and not too dry.

RISO AL POMODORO, ALL'OLIO O IN BRODO

Rice with tomato, oil, or in stock

Rice, 300 g - Salt

We summarize these three recipes in only one because their simplicity. Rice with tomato: boil the rice in lightly salted water and season it with hot tomato sauce (see recipe) and roughly chopped basil leaves, and if you like, add a sprinkle of red chili pepper. Rice with oil: season the rice with plenty of excellent olive oil, and, if you like, add a sprinkle of black pepper. Rice in stock: simply boil the rice in vegetable stock (see recipe).

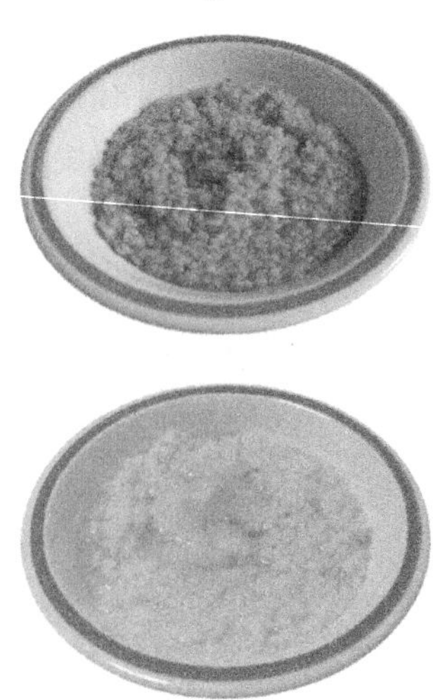

SPAGHETTI AGLIO, OLIO E PEPERONCINO

Garlic, oil and chili pepper spaghetti

Spaghetti, 250 g - 1 garlic clove - 4 red hot chili peppers
Olive oil - Salt

Put a pot with enough salted water to cook the spaghetti over the heat. Fry gently the garlic and the chilies (with seeds removed) finely chopped in oil generously poured, but do not overdo, into a pan of appropriate size. Once you drain the spaghetti "al dente", transfer them to the pan over a high heat, stirring, and letting them flavor.

Who does not like garlic can put it whole to fry in oil and remove it prior to season the pasta. We remember that spaghetti should not be broken, but put in the pot resting on the edges: as they soften them slide down into the boiling water by themselves, with the help of a fork if necessary.

TORTELLI DI PATATE[6]

Potato "tortelli"

Flour, 400 g (in addition to that required for preparation)
4 medium floury potatoes - A sprig of parsley - Salt and pepper

Prepare the dough on the floured pastry board by mixing the flour with a pinch of salt and sufficient water to make the

---

[6] A traditional seasoning is butter and sage, vegans can use, for example, soy butter instead of the cow's one: fry a few sage leaves in the butter for a few minutes, and pour over the tortelli. Another seasoning par excellence is meat sauce whose vegan version is not however here contemplated.

dough elastic and homogeneous. Give it the shape of a ball, and leave it to rest in a cloth in a cool place.

Meanwhile, boil the potatoes for the filling. Peel them still hot, and mix with the chopped parsley, salt and pepper. If the filling left over, do not worry: it is good to eat just as it is!

Roll out the dough and cut it into not too thin strips, about double the width of the future tortelli, i.e.10 cm, then sprinkle with flour. Pick up a small ball of filling and lay down it on one side of the strip of pasta, then dispose the other balls at regular distances on the strips. Overlap the other flap of the strip and press the edges with a fork to seal them, and then cut the tortelli with a pastry wheel. Place them side by side on a slightly floured cloth. Boil the tortelli in lightly salted boiling water for 5 minutes, taking them up with a skimmer when they come up to the surface. A good seasoning is tomato sauce (see recipe).

ZUPPA DI CIPOLLE
Onion soup

6 red onions - 4 slices of stale homemade bread
Olive oil - Salt end pepper

Put the onions chopped into thin slices in oil in a pan. Let them sweat over a low heat, and stir. When withdrawn, add some hot water, and keep cooking for at least an hour. Dose salt and pepper. Toast the slices of bread, place them in the bowls and pour over the hot soup.

To give more flavor to the course you can add some vegetable stock instead of water. If you wish, you can also use white onions, or leeks, instead red onions.

ZUPPA LOMBARDA
"Lombard" bread and bean soup

Boiled white beans, 500 g - 4 slices of stale homemade bread
Olive oil - Salt and pepper

Boil the beans with a sprig of sage following the recipe for *beans in oil.* Toast the slices of bread, put them in the bowls and pour over the hot cooking stock of the beans with a few of beans themselves and a sage leaf. Season with plenty of excellent oil, salt and pepper.

VEGETABLE DISHES AND GARNISHES

BUGLIONE DI ZUCCHINE

Courgette soup

12 courgettes (zucchini) - Half an onion - 1 artichoke (optional)
Tomato pulp, 100 g - Olive oil - Salt and pepper

Slice the courgettes and put them to fry in a pan with 4 tablespoons of oil along with the onion not too fine chopped (a leek can also fit) and, if desired, also an artichoke deprived of the hardest leaves. Add a few tablespoons of tomato, dosing salt and pepper, and leave to cook slowly for about half an hour.

CARCIOFI FRITTI[7]

Fried artichokes

4 artichokes - Flour, 150 g - Olive oil - Salt

Artichokes, whatever the recipe, must be dipped for a few minutes in water made acidic with lemon juice to avoid oxidation, drained and

---

7 See the recipe of fiori di zucca fritti.

dried properly so they do not retain too much moisture among the bracts.

Remove the stems and the tough outer leaves of the artichokes, trim the ends and cut them vertically in four quarters. Make a batter with water and flour, and dip the artichokes into it. Fry a few at a time in plenty of hot oil, removing them with a perforated spatula. Set to dry on absorbent kitchen paper, salting. They are enjoyed hot, but they are good even cold.

CARCIOFI RIFATTI

Reheated artichokes

4 artichokes - 1 garlic clove
Parsley - Olive oil
Salt and pepper

Remove the stems of the acidic artichokes (see previous recipe), leaving a small part cleaned of hair, trim the ends and cut vertically into four quarters. Chop garlic and parsley and put everything to cook in a pan with oil for about a quarter of an hour.

CARCIOFI RIPIENI[8]

Stuffed artichokes

4 artichokes - 1 garlic clove - Parsley - Breadcrumbs - Olive oil
Salt and pepper

Remove the stems of the acidic artichokes (see previous recipe), trim the ends and remove empty the innermost leaves, leaving a cavity to be filled with the filling. For the latter you proceed as for stuffed tomatoes (see recipe).

CAROTE IN TEGAME

Carrots in pan

12 carrots - A sprig of sage - Olive oil - Salt and pepper

Wash the carrots, and cut them into slices. Cook into a pan with oil, sage, and salt until they are soft. If you like, a sprinkle of black pepper.

CAVOLFIORE FRITTO[9]

Fried cauliflower

1 cauliflower - Flour, as required - Olive oil - Salt

Parboil the cauliflower in boiling water for less time than it takes to be completely boiled. Divide the cauliflower ball into florets, dip them in a batter made with flour and water and a

---

[8] The traditional recipe requires a filling made from beef.

[9] See the recipe of fiori di zucca fritti.

pinch of salt, and fry in hot oil. Set on absorbent kitchen paper, salting.

CAVOLFIORE LESSO

Boiled cauliflower

1 cauliflower - 1 lemon
Olive oil - Salt and pepper

Boil the whole cauliflower for about half an hour in salted water, starting from the boil, until it can be pierced with a fork without resistance. Divide the ball into florets and season with oil, lemon, pepper, and salt if necessary. It is good either hot or cold.

CAVOLFIORE STRASCICATO[10]

Dragged cauliflower

1 cauliflower - 2 garlic cloves - 1 floret (or seeds) of wild fennel
Tomato pulp (see below) - Olive oil - Salt and pepper

Why "dragged" cauliflower? Because it seems literally "dragged" through the tomato sauce to be dressed!

---

[10] In this vegan version sausages are missing. However in our opinion, the taste of the dish is not affected much.

Divide the cauliflower into florets, and put them into a pan with oil, garlic, fennel and a tablespoon of tomato pulp. If there are also some leaves attached to the ball of cauliflower do not throw away, but add them too because they enrich the course.

FAGIOLI ALL'OLIO

Beans in oil

Beans, 500 g (200 g if dried)
1 garlic clove - Sage
Olive oil
Salt and pepper

If the beans are dried they have to be previously soaked for half a day and in weight they have to be a little less than a half of what is required if they are fresh. Put the beans with garlic and some sage leaves to boil slowly in salted water, starting from cold, for about 2 hours. Keep the pot closed with the lid. Take care that the boil occurs at a very low heat, so that the skin of the beans breaks to the minimum. Once cooked, drain the beans and season with plenty of oil, salt and pepper.

They are delicious either hot or cold, but hot they give of their best. In the same way you can prepare chickpeas in oil, *which are not less good.*

FAGIOLI ALL'UCCELLETTO

Beans with tomato

Boiled cannellini beans, 500 g - 3 garlic cloves
Tomato pulp, 100 g - Sage - Olive oil - Salt and pepper

To boil the beans follow previous recipe. Put the garlic in the oil to golden, then add the beans, tomato pulp and sage, and cook slowly for about a quarter of an hour.

FAGIOLI E CIPOLLE[11]

Beans and onion

Boiled white beans, 400 g - 4 white onions - Olive oil - Salt and pepper

Boil the beans according to the recipe for *beans in oil.* Add the chopped onions and season with oil, salt and pepper. Simple, but great!

---

[11] This recipe is simply what remains of beans, tuna and onions when tuna is missing.

The onion can also be red, but white onions are really ideal.

FAGIOLINI VERDI AL POMODORO

Runner beans with tomato

Runner beans, 400 g - Tomato pulp, 200 g - 1 garlic clove
Olive oil - Salt

Put the garlic to golden in a pan with 3 tablespoons of oil, add tomato pulp and the beans which have been previously trimmed and washed. The cooking takes about half an hour. Add the salt.

FAGIOLINI VERDI LESSI

Boiled runner beans

Runner beans, 400 g - 1 garlic clove - 1 lemon - Olive oil - Salt

Trim the ends of the beans and wash them. Boil by immersing in boiling salted water and leave not for too long, until they can be pierced by with fork without resistance. At the end of boiling they should be still nicely green, not wilted, and rich in flavor. Season with oil, finely chopped garlic and lemon juice.

FINOCCHI RIFATTI
Fennels

2 large fennels - 2 garlic cloves
Sage - Olive oil
Salt and pepper

For this course, it is better to prefer the large fennels than the smaller ones. Put the garlic cloves and the sage to sweat in oil in a pan. Wash the fennels, remove the stems and the green leaves, and slice vertically along the veins. Add a little water and leave to cook for about half an hour.

INSALATA
Salad

Salad vegetables - Lemon juice
1 garlic clove - Olive oil - Vinegar
Salt and pepper

Wash the vegetables leaves one by one, drain, and if you want, you can break them with hands. Place into a tureen and season with plenty of oil, lemon juice, salt. Optionally, you can add a garlic clove finely chopped, pepper, and vinegar. Use your taste to combine the varieties of vegetables and the condiments.

MELANZANE AL POMODORO[12]
Aubergines in tomato

4 medium aubergines - 2 garlic cloves
Tomato pulp, 250 g - Basil
Grated Parmesan cheese - Olive oil
Fine and coarse salt, pepper

Cut the aubergines into slices, and put them in a tray and sprinkle with coarse salt. Keep them for about 2 hours under the pressure of another plate with a weight on it to expel the vegetation water. Remove the salt by washing, dry well and lightly fry in a pan with some oil, then place on absorbent kitchen paper to dry. Cook them in another pan with garlic, chopped basil, tomato pulp and oil for about half an hour, adjust salt and pepper.

---

[12] This is the vegan version of the well known aubergines parmigiana, made with Parmesan cheese.

**This is the vegan version of the well known aubergines parmigiana, made with Parmesan cheese.*

MELANZANE FRITTE

Fried aubergines

4 medium aubergines - Flour, 200 g - Olive oil for frying
Fine and coarse salt

Apply to the aubergines the same treatment described in the previous recipe to take away their acidity. Remove the salt, dredge in flour and fry a few at a time in plenty of hot oil until they are golden. Put them on adsorbent kitchen paper to dry the excess oil. We recommend not peeling the aubergines.

PATATE ALLA CONTADINA

Potatoes farmer style

Potatoes, 800 g - Tomato preserve (see recipe) - Fennel seeds
Olive oil - Salt and pepper

Peel the potatoes, cut them into chunks and place in a pot with a tablespoon of tomato preserve, a pinch of fennel seeds, olive oil, salt and pepper. Cover all with water and put the pot over the heat until you can pierce the potatoes with a fork without resistance. You may need to add more water during the cooking.

If you do not like fennel you can replace it with rosemary or sage.

PATATE ARROSTO
Roasted potatoes

Potatoes, 800 g - 2 garlic cloves
Sage - Rosemary - Olive oil - Salt and pepper

Chop the potatoes into chunks, and place into a pan with oil, the other herbs and salt on the heat, or bake. Stir frequently to prevent sticking on the bottom of the pan. After cooking, the potatoes should be well browned outside, and soft and juicy inside. If you like, sprinkle with pepper.

Also good are potatoes backed under ashes (for those who have a fireplace), as my Mother, who comes from the slopes of Tuscan-Romagnolo Apennines, remembers: the potatoes are covered with ashes mixed with burning embers, then they are peeled and seasoned in one of the many possible ways.

PATATE FRITTE
Fried potatoes

Yellow potatoes, 700 g - Sage - Olive oil for frying - Salt

Peel the potatoes, cut them into pieces no more half a cm thick, and fry a few at a time in plenty of hot oil. Along with fried potatoes you can also fry beautiful sage leaves that will become very crisp and crumbly. Salt them after frying, place on absorbent kitchen paper and eat hot.

PATATE LESSE

Boiled potatoes

Potatoes, 800 g - 2 garlic cloves
Parsley - Olive oil
Salt and pepper

Boil the potatoes, peel while still warm and cut into chunks. Season with chopped garlic and parsley, plenty of oil, and salt. If you like, add black pepper.

PEPERONATA
Peppers

4 red and yellow peppers
1 onion - Tomato pulp, 250 g
Olive oil - Salt

Cut the peppers into not too big strips, and put them to cook with oil, tomato pulp, onion chopped into slices, and salt. Cooking takes about half an hour and ends when the peppers are completely withered.

PISELLI ALLA FIORENTINA[13]
Florentine peas

Peas, 600 g - 4 garlic cloves
Sugar - Olive oil - Salt

Put the garlic to brown in oil in a saucepan. After a few minutes, add the raw peas, a teaspoon of sugar and a little hot water or vegetable stock. After a quarter of an hour the peas are ready and they can be salted just before the end of cooking.

---

[13] The traditional recipe requires carnesecca (bacon).

POLENTA FRITTA
Fried cornmeal

Cornmeal, 500 g (see recipe)
Olive oil for frying - Salt

For the preparation of cornmeal follow the recipe. Cut it into slices not too high and then into small rectangles, then fry in plenty of hot oil. Let them dry in absorbent kitchen paper, salt and enjoy.

From this recipe and sautéed porcino mushrooms (see recipe) you can prepare excellent polenta croutons with porcini mushrooms to serve as a starter simply deposing a little of mushrooms on each slice of polenta.

POLPETTE DI PATATE[14]
Potato balls

Boiled potatoes, 500 g - 1 garlic clove
Breadcrumbs, 150 g - Parsley - Basil
Olive oil for frying - Salt

[14] The traditional recipe requires egg yolk and grated Parmesan cheese.

Chop garlic, basil and parsley. Mix the peeled potatoes adding the chopped herb, the garlic and salt, and form the mixture into small round balls a little flat. Coat in breadcrumbs and fry until nicely golden. Let them dry on absorbent kitchen paper, salt and enjoy.

POMODORI GRATINATI

Grilled tomatoes

4 ripe salad tomatoes - 1 garlic clove - Parsley
Breadcrumbs, 100 g - Olive oil
Salt and pepper

Cut the tomatoes in two horizontally and remove the seeds. Oil the tomatoes and sprinkle with breadcrumbs and chopped garlic and parsley. Place them on the grill, adjusting salt and pepper: As they are well withered they are ready.

POMODORI RIPIENI

Stuffed tomatoes

4 ripe salad tomatoes - 1 garlic clove
Parsley - Breadcrumbs
Olive oil - Salt and pepper

Cut the tomatoes in half horizontally and remove the seeds. Prepare the filling with chopped garlic, parsley, salt and pepper, to which you can add some breadcrumbs to give it more volume and texture. Fill the half tomatoes and put them to cook in a pan with a little oil over low heat until the skin is well withered. You can also make *stuffed onions* following the same recipe.

An alternative filling is made with boiled rice combined with the usual odors chopped.

Following the same preparation you can make even stuffed onions.

PORCINI ALLA BRACE

Grilled porcino mushrooms

Porcino mushrooms (caps only), 500 g
2 garlic cloves - Olive oil
Salt and pepper

For this course, use only the caps of the mushrooms, so when you buy them you should choose those with large caps. The stems can be reused for other courses, such as sautéed porcino mushrooms (see recipe).

Clean always wild mushrooms from the woods (unlike champignon) only by dusting and moistening, without washing them. Take the caps, make some cuts on the top, and put into them some small slices of garlic, salt and roast them on the grill top and bottom. If you like, a little oil after cooking.

PORCINI FRITTI

Fried porcino mushrooms

Porcino mushrooms (caps only), 500 g - Flour, 150 g
Olive oil for frying - Salt

For this recipe too it is better use large porcino mushrooms. Slice both the caps and the stems, dredge in flour, and fry a few at a time in hot oil. Note that the frying has to be very alive but very short. Drain, dry on kitchen paper and salt: they are amazing eaten hot.

PORCINI TRIFOLATI

Sautéed porcino mushrooms

Porcino mushrooms, 500 g - 2 garlic cloves - Catmint - Olive oil
Salt

For this recipe is not necessary to use large and well formed mushrooms. Chop both the caps and the stems in not too small pieces and put them to cook in a pan with garlic, catmint leaves and oil for about 10 minutes. Of course, you can also prepare other varieties of mushrooms in this way.

PURE' DI PAPATE[15]

Mashed potatoes

Potatoes, 500 g - Vegetable butter, 40 g
Vegetable milk, 2 dl
Salt

Boil the potatoes, peel and pass them through a food mill. Put them in a saucepan with the butter and the milk. Stir continuously until you get a creamy mixture: in the meantime salt.

VALIGETTE DI VARZA[16]

Savoy cabbage cases

Half a savoy cabbage - 2 courgettes
Tomato pulp, 150 g
Leftover vegetables
Olive oil - Salt

Cut the courgettes into thin slices and brown in oil. Add tomato pulp, the courgettes and the leftover vegetables crushing everything with a little oil and salt until you have a sort of mush. Prepare the "cases" with large cabbage leaves that you have previously blanched slightly, on which you lay a layer of the mush. Roll everything up, and fasten with some toothpicks. Finally, finish the cooking of the "cases" in a pan with 3 tablespoons of oil.

---

[15] The traditional recipe requires cow's milk and butter.

[16] In the traditional recipe also leftovers of meats, cold cuts and cheeses are used.

The secret and the usefulness of the "cases" is that leftover vegetables can be reused to make the filling.

HOW TO BOIL VEGETABLES

Clean and wash the vegetables as needed: boil them in salted water already boiling until "al dente", not overcooking, so that they retain their entire flavor. Obviously, the time depends on the type of vegetable. Furthermore, the cooking water should be the minimum sufficient quantity, in order not to unnecessarily absorb the substance from vegetables. If the water reduces during boiling, add other boiling water from a separate saucepan. Season the boiled vegetables with plenty of excellent olive oil and salt.

A trick to boil courgettes is to cut them into small pieces before: in this way the boiling time will be shorter than that for whole courgettes, and so the taste will be better preserved. Trying is believing!

VERDURE RIFATTE

Reheated vegetables

Boiled vegetables (spinach, chard, chicory, herbs, turnips, etc.), 500 g - 2 garlic cloves - Olive oil - Salt

Boil the vegetables following the previous recipe: sauté briefly in oil over high heat with slices of garlic already browned. Salt.

In order to fully enjoy the aroma of each variety of vegetables, we suggest to "reheat" one at a time.

ZUCCHINE RIPIENE[17]

Stuffed courgettes

8 round courgettes (zucchini) - 1 onion
1 garlic clove - Tomato pulp - Basil
Parsley - Breadcrumbs - Soft inside of bread
Bread crumb - Olive oil - Salt

Open the courgettes by cutting a slice horizontally near the top, and empty them inside with a teaspoon. Prepare the filling with crumbled soft inside of bread, part of the courgettes pulp, basil, parsley, garlic, salt and pepper. Fill the courgettes finishing the filling with a layer of breadcrumbs and then close them with their "hat". Begin cooking in oil with some chopped onion, add tomato pulp and water gradually to prevent sticking: adjust the salt.

---

[17] In the traditional recipe the filling is made from beef.

CAKES, SWEETMEATS, ETC.

BALLOTTE

Boiled chestnut

Chestnuts, 1 kg , A floret of fennel , Salt

Peel the chestnuts and boil them for about one hour and a half with a sprig of fennel and a little salt. When they are sufficiently cooled, but still warm, remove the inner membrane, and enjoy. They are good either hot or cold.

BRUCIATE

Roast chestnuts

Chestnuts, 1 kg

Make a small cut on the skin of the chestnuts to prevent bursting during roasting and to facilitate the shelling. Then place them in the apposite perforated pan, and put on the grill. Who does not have access to a fireplace, can anyway use the gas stove. After about 20 minutes, when the skin is well browned, remove from heat and peel. They give the best eaten still hot. Grappa is an excellent accompaniment.

BUDINO DI RISO[18]

Rice pudding

Rice for cakes, 250 g - Rice milk, 1 l - Sugar, 100 g
Soy butter, 30 g - Grated rinds of 1 lemon and 1 orange
Powdered sugar - Breadcrumbs - Cornstarch, a tablespoon

Boil the rice in the milk with the sugar for about half an hour. When cooked, add the butter or the oil, the grated rinds and the cornstarch, stirring well. Grease a cake pan or some smaller molds for cakes (typically of oval shape) with butter or oil, sprinkle with breadcrumbs, and pour the mixture into it. Bake at 200° for about half an hour, taking care that the outer surface of the pudding does not darken. When cooked, sprinkle with powdered sugar.

CASTAGNACCIO

Chestnut cake

Sweet chestnut flour, 400 g - Pine nuts, 50 g - Walnuts, 50 g
Rosemary - Olive oil - Salt

This cake is also known by the name "migliaccio", and it is traditionally prepared in autumn, as the chestnut flour has just out of the mill. Mix the flour with water and add a pinch of salt:

---

[18] Soy butter and rise milk are in place of the cow's ones, and eggs have been eliminated. Soy butter may be validly replaced by olive oil.

the mixture should be quite firm. Disseminate the mixture of pine nuts, crushed walnuts and a pinch of rosemary needles. Roll out the mixture into a well oiled low rectangular pan, so that it is high about 1 cm. Bake in the preheated oven at 200 ° C for half an hour.

CENCI[19]

Rags

Flour, 300 g - 2 spoonfuls of sugar
Soy butter, 50 g - Powdered sugar
Olive oil for frying - Salt

The rags are traditionally prepared during Carnival. Mix the flour, the sugar and the butter (not cold and semi melted) with a pinch of salt, making a well mixed dough. Let it stand for an hour, then roll out fairly fine, and cut into some slightly irregular pieces. Curl them like butterflies, and fry in plenty of hot oil, until they are crispy on the outside but soft on the inside. Place them on kitchen paper and sprinkle with powdered sugar (if it is not available, you can use ordinary sugar).

[19] Soy butter is in place of the cow's one, and eggs have been eliminated. Soy butter may be validly replaced by olive oil.

FICATTOLE

Fried dough

Flour, 300 g - Brewer's yeast, 20 g - Sugar (or fine salt)
Olive oil for frying

Dissolve the yeast in water and pour it into the flour, adding a tablespoon of oil. Cover the dough with a cloth and let it rise for 2 hours. If you do not want to prepare by yourself the dough, you can buy it already prepared. Roll out the dough not too thin, cut into small rhombuses, and fry in hot oil. Arrange the pastries on kitchen paper and at this point you can choose to sprinkle with plenty of sugar or a little salt. If you choose salt, ficattole can be a great accompaniment to many salted courses

Although they are not a recipe, the author wants to remember among the sweet recipes some pastries made by Nature itself, where the only human contribution is drying: ***dried figs****.*

FRAGOLE AL VINO ROSSO

Strawberries in red wine

Strawberries, 500 g - Fruity red wine, ½ l - Sugar, 100 g

Wash the strawberries and remove petioles and leaves. Cut them in half if they are small and in several pieces if they are larger. Soak them in red wine, and sprinkle with sugar. Put in the fridge, and serve cool.

FIRTTELLE DI FARINA DOLCE

Sweet flour fritters

Sweet chestnut flour, 500 g - Sugar
Olive oil for frying
Salt

Dissolve the chestnut flour in cold water with a pinch of salt until the mixture is quite liquid. Take the mixture with a tablespoon and, spoonful by spoonful, fry in hot oil. When the frying is finished, lay the fritters on kitchen paper, and sprinkle with sugar.

FRITTELLE DI MELE

Apple fritters

4 apples - Flour, 100 g - Sugar, 100 g
Olive oil for frying

Prepare a not too liquid batter with flour and water. Remove the core of the apples with the corer, and cut them horizontally into slices about half a cm high. Dip in the batter and fry in hot oil. Place the fritters on kitchen paper and sprinkle with plenty of sugar.

Typically, these fritters are made with renette apples, but you can also try with other varieties.

FRITTELLE DI RISO[20]

Rice fritters

Rice for cakes, 400 g - Sugar, 400 g - 1 orange
Vegetable milk, 1 l - Flour
Olive oil for frying - Salt

Rice fritters are traditionally prepared for the feast of St. Giovanni which falls on March 19. Boil the rice in the milk and add half the sugar when the boil is arisen. Mix the rice with the juice of the orange, and a pinch of salt. If the consistency of the dough is not sufficient, add some flour. Fry the mixture in small portions, using with a wet tablespoon, in plenty of hot oil. Once fried, dispose the fritters on kitchen paper, and sprinkle with plenty of sugar.

LIQUORE DI MORE

Blackberry liquor

Ripe blackberries, 1 kg - Sugar, 500 g
Alcohol at 90°, 2 l

Wash the blackberries, boil without water until they are almost macerated, and add the sugar. Continue boiling until

[20] Cow's milk is in place of the rice one, and eggs have been eliminated.

you have a mush. Spread a clean linen cloth into a container of adequate size, pour in the mush and close the cloth like a candy. Squeeze the "candy", and collect the filtered liquid in the container. Finally, add the alcohol, stir and hermetically seal the liquor in one or more bottles.

MARMELLATA DI MORE
Blackberry jam

Blackberries, 1 kg - Sugar, 500 g

Going for picking blackberries in the summer can be an opportunity for some good outings: collect only those that are beautiful, soft and ripe, and not those that are still partially green. Wash the blackberries, boil without water until they are almost macerated, and add the sugar. Continue boiling until you have a mush, and then pass it through a food mill. Put the jam into jars while it is still hot, so that the cooling creates a "vacuum", and hermetically seal the jars. After you have opened a jar, you will have to store it in the fridge.

MELE COTTE
Cooked apples

4 apples (renette or Granny Smith) - Sugar

Put the apples to boil in half a cm water in a pot with a lid, so that the heat and the steam do not escape, and they distribute around the apples, cooking them from all sides. Add some sugar on the apples when the skin begins to crack. The cooking time depends on the type of apple, but on average is about 20 minutes. Likewise, you can also cook pears.

PAN DI RAMERINO

Rosemary bread

Flour, 350 g - Sugar, 50 g
Brewer's yeast, 20 g
Sultanas, 100 g
Olive oil
Salt

Rosemary bread is traditionally prepared on Holy Thursday of the Easter time. Mix the flour with water, the yeast dissolved in water in a bowl, sugar and a pinch of salt. Cover the dough with a cloth and let it rise for an hour. Get back to knead the dough adding 3 tablespoons of oil, the sultanas and a generous pinch of rosemary needles. Make 4 round loaves, make 4 incisions onto each (like a sharp, for who knows musical notation), and let them rise a little longer. Finally, bake at 200 ° C for half an hour.

PANE, BURRO E ZUCCHERO[21]

Butter and sugar bread

4 slices of fresh homemade bread - Soy butter - Sugar (or fine salt)

Spread the soy butter on the bread slices, and sprinkle with plenty of sugar (or a pinch of salt).

PANE, VINO E ZUCCHERO

Wine and sugar bread

4 slices of fresh homemade bread - Red wine - Sugar

Pour the red wine onto the brad slices, and sprinkle with plenty of sugar.

---

[21] Cow's butter has been substituted with the soy one. You may also try other varieties of vegetable butter.

SCHIACCIATA ALLA FIORENTINA[22]

Florentine flat cake

In this case, we do not give the amounts in grams (except butter and yeast), but just as they were transmitted to the author.

12 spoonfuls of flour - 10 of rice milk - 8 of sugar
4 of olive oil - 1 orange - Brewer's yeast, 20 g - Icing sugar
Soy butter, 20 g - Salt

Florentine flat cake is traditionally prepared during Carnival. Grate the zest of the orange. Make a mixture in a bowl with the flour, the sugar, the milk, the oil, the grated zest, the orange juice, the yeast and a pinch of salt, and let it rest for about an hour. Pour the mixture into a rectangular pan greased with the butter: to prevent the flat cake from sticking to the pan, you can use the trick of dusting the bottom of the pan with bread crumbs. Bake at 200 ° C for half an hour. When cooked, sprinkle the flat cake with plenty of icing sugar.

Traditionally, people use to put over the flat cake a stencil in the shape of the Florence's lily, in order to leave the design impressed after the dusting with icing sugar.

---

[22] Cow's milk and butter have been substitute with the rise and the soy ones respectively.

SCHIACCIATA CON L'UVA

Flat cake with grapes

Wine grapes, 600 g - Flour, 250 g - Sugar, 100 g
Brewer's yeast, 15 g - Rosemary - Olive oil - Salt

Flat cake with grapes is prepared in the autumn at the grape harvest time. If you do not want to prepare the bread dough by yourself, you can buy 800 g already prepared. Otherwise, mix the flour with water and the yeast, previously dissolved in water, in a bowl. Cover the dough with a cloth and let it rise for one hour. Knead the dough again, adding half the sugar, a tablespoon of oil and a pinch of salt.

Grease a rectangular pan, and roll out half of the dough, making sure it raises over the edges by about 1 cm. Remove the grapes from the bunches, wash them, let them dry and spread a half over the dough, crushing them a little. Sprinkle with the sugar and pour a little oil. With the rest of the dough make a second layer, and lay it down over the first one, pressing with the fingers. Repeat the same steps made with the first layer with grapes, sugar and oil, and add a pinch of rosemary leaves. Let it rise for another hour and bake at 200 ° C for half an hour.

Stretta la foglia, larga la via, dite la vostra che ho detto la mia.

The leaf is narrow, the road is large, say your since I said mine.

Printed in Great Britain
by Amazon

Fabrizio Baroni

My Grandma's *Vegan* Recipes

85 traditional Tuscan dishes to keep healthy and relish all year round

All the photographs of the author

Copyright © 2016 FABRIZIO BARONI
Via Antonio del Pollaiolo 89
Florence, Italy 50142
baronifab@libero.it

All rights reserved

ISBN-10: 1537328735
ISBN-13: 978-1537328737